before &after
decorating

welcome

Better Homes and Gardens® Creative Collection™

Director, Editorial Administration
Michael L. Maine

Editor-in-Chief
Beverly Rivers

Executive Editor	Karman Wittry Hotchkiss

Editorial Manager	**Art Director**
Ann Blevins	Brenda Drake Lesch

Copy Chief	Mary Heaton
Administrative Assistant	Lori Eggers
Contributing Editor	Jody Garlock
Contributing Graphic Designer	Tracy DeVenney
Contributing Copy Editor	Dave Kirchner
Contributing Photographers	Craig Anderson, King Au, Gordon Beall, Ross Chapple, Michael Garland

Vice President, Publishing Director
William R. Reed

Group Publisher	Steve Levinson
Senior Marketing Manager	Suzy Johnson

Chairman and CEO
William T. Kerr

In Memoriam
E. T. Meredith III (1933-2003)

Publishing Group President
Stephen M. Lacy
Magazine Group President
Jack Griffin
Publishing Group Executive Vice President
Jerry Kaplan

Have you been wondering what to do about the bland walls in your bedroom? Are you at a loss when it comes to ideas for decorating your living room? Perhaps you're ready to make your home office really work for you. Or maybe you want to finally give your teen's bedroom a boost. You've come to the right place! *Before & After Decorating* is packed with ideas and inspiration for turning blah rooms into beauties.

The transformations in *Before & After Decorating* are taken from stories of real homeowners faced with common decorating dilemmas, be it uninspired furnishings, lifeless walls, or clutter run amok. Unlike high-end design magazines where rooms go from pretty to prettier, these rooms lacked charisma. Just check out the "before" photos to see what we mean. You'll discover a spartan dining room—it had nothing in it other than a table and chairs—transformed into a divine eating space. You'll witness how a cluttered home office, which actually was a seldom-used living room, was turned into a functional and stylish work space. You'll also glimpse revivals of bedrooms, a living room, a sunroom, and an attic. And you'll meet many of the homeowners who gained the confidence to tackle other rooms in their homes.

There's more, too. From choosing furnishings and window treatments to stenciling and budget-friendly artwork, you'll discover projects that are easy to complete and ideas you can apply to your own home. Many of the techniques used are summarized at the end of each story, along with design tips to give you the know-how to proceed.

Read on and get inspired. Before you start your own room makeover, though, be sure to snap some photos so you can look back on the amazing transformation.

Happy Decorating!

contents

the romance of it all

A lifeless dining room gains a sense of grandeur that makes it worthy of quiet candlelit dinners.

before

Andee and Barry Walden's 4-year-old home has a combined dining room and living room. That meant that the dining room needed to remain neutral to allow design latitude in the living room. Columns defined the two areas, but they were stark white pillars until they got a faux-marble paint treatment.

THIS PHOTO: Luscious fabrics and layering give the room a cozy quality. Trims, such as tassels, beads, and fringe, offer flirty flourishes. Dressed with a gracious swag, flowing panels, and pearl-studded sheers, the bay window is now an attention-getter.
BELOW RIGHT: Snake grass sprouting from vases adds striking contemporary flair to a traditional vignette atop the antique sideboard.

Aside from an antique table and chairs, the dining room in Andee and Barry Walden's Maryland home didn't have much going for it. Walls were bare, a bay window lacked drama, and the chandelier that hung over the table was a typical home-center variety. It's no wonder, then, that Andee still marvels at the transformation that took place in her home in just a few short days. The formerly lackluster dining room emerged as an elegant and romantic space for entertaining. "It was more fun than Christmas," Andee says of the makeover. "Everything was just gorgeous, and I could hardly wait for it all to come together."

The whirlwind redo started when room decorators Wanda Ventling and Becky Lau Ekstrand—armed with fabric and wallpaper samples—toured the room after a phone conversation with Andee. "I can't believe that they could find out so much about me and my tastes in a phone conversation," Andee says. "They came with just the perfect ideas. I loved them all."

At the home, the decorating team found challenges that are universal: The space is a combination living room and dining room, so maintaining a separate identity but easy flow was key. The Waldens, who have two toddlers, wanted the room to be both adultlike and child-friendly—goals that seemed at odds. "I like the traditional/eclectic look with formal flair yet with a touch of casualness," Andee says. "I wanted the space to be inviting and cozy not intimidating."

The plan the decorators presented to Andee met her needs to a tee. In fabrics, furnishings, and accessories, they mixed traditional with contemporary and formal with casual. The existing chairs would be updated with new upholstery,

and an antique sideboard would be brought in to complement the dining set. Shades of green—Andee's favorite color—were chosen for their timeless appeal.

After the decorating team's visit, Andee and Barry awaited the next phase. Barry, an aerospace engineer, moved the ceiling wiring in anticipation of the new chandelier. Shipments of furniture and accessories begged to be opened and examined, and workers began to arrive. Painting and wallpapering contractors worked wonders on the stark ceiling, the walls, and the two columns that separated the dining room from the living area. Three distinct styles of wallpaper, ranging from a contemporary leaf design to a traditional pattern, were hung in unexpected ways on the ceiling and in panels on the lower walls to mimic wainscoting. All of the papers have metallic accents or texture, lending additional visual interest. For continuity, the wallpaper was extended into the living room.

When the decorators returned for four days of hard work, Andee was eager for the fun to begin. They removed the worn fabric from the chairs and reupholstered them, hung draperies to give the bay window presence, stitched table runners, embellished plain candles, and accessorized until they hit just the right note of casual elegance.

As with any decorating project, there were a few glitches along the way. The drapery rods the decorators had ordered arrived broken, so the team had to come up with a spur-of-the-moment alternative. Because the bay window was wide—it spanned 110 inches—finding a ready-made rod locally was impossible. Undaunted,

OPPOSITE: The crystal chandelier, one of the big splurges in the room, is an impressive replacement for the original fixture that was too small in scale for the space. On one wall, the arms of two pairs of sconces become creative brackets for displaying platters. BELOW LEFT: Crystal, roses, and candles create a formal table setting. Many of the candles in the room were embellished with paint to create a custom look on a budget. BELOW: A heavy-duty olefin fabric replaced the upholstery on Andee's antique chairs, making them nearly childproof.

the decorators improvised by combining two shorter metal rods into one, proving that there's a creative solution to every design challenge.

For Andee, the biggest challenge came the night before the room was photographed. She and her sister decided to sew tiny pearls to the sheers on the bay window. "It seemed like a small task, but once we started, we realized we'd never get the job done in time," she says. Andee called the lead decorator in a panic. A hot-glue gun solved the problem—at least temporarily, until the photography was completed and Andee could sew the beads in place so her boys wouldn't pull them off and swallow them.

Andee says she learned much about interior design during her crash course. "I am an engineer by training, and I tend to think in a linear, one-dimensional mode," she says. "The designers taught me to think outside the box and into the next dimension." The creative combination and use of the wallpapers, for example, is something Andee says never would have crossed her mind.

With one room under her belt, Andee now has the confidence to forge ahead on her own by decorating other rooms in her home. "We can see the foyer from the dining room, and it looks so drab now," she says. "The designers have shown me that I can tackle decorating that area. I can envision how I want it to look, so that's my next project."

ABOVE: Often overlooked for decorating potential, the ceiling can brim with style by adding wallpaper framed with molding strips. BELOW: A new wool rug is perfectly sized for the room. It accommodates all of the chairs, even when they're pulled away from the table. RIGHT: Rod-pocket panels hung on decorative rods and tied back with garlands lend extra definition between the two rooms. Swing-arm rods outfitted with panels also would create soft separation between two spaces.

ABOVE: Barry and Andee, with sons Micah and Joshua, enjoy the fruits of their labors. ABOVE RIGHT: The window treatment consists of a self-lined swag draped over a rod and side panels attached to the wall. Sheers hang beneath to softly diffuse light. RIGHT: Informal, neutral-color pottery is inexpensive enough that Andee won't feel uncomfortable when the children use it. Fresh fruit—in this case, gilded pears with leaf-shape name tags—makes simple yet striking place markers.

"Now that the room is finished, I can imagine us sitting down to a nice, quiet dinner," Andee says.

the decorators' plan

1. Measure the room, windows, and doors. Draw an accurate floor plan. We also measured the dining table and chairs.

2. Develop a plan to maximize the room's function. We added chairs and a sideboard to increase seating and serving space. The palette can be adapted to the season.

3. Purchase furniture. We found a sideboard for less than $600 at a local antiques shop. We also purchased two Parsons chairs.

4. Empty the room of furniture. We also had the homeowner remove a ceiling light fixture and move the wiring to allow for a centered fixture.

5. Paint the ceiling and molding. We had a paint store match the off-white background of one of the wallpapers. We used the table's dimensions to help determine the dimensions of the ceiling treatment, and installed the wallpapers and moldings accordingly.

6. Paint the walls and columns. A faux-marble paint treatment dresses up the columns. We then wallpapered some of the walls, repeating the papers used for the ceiling.

7. Re-cover the chairs. We found a stain-resistant chenille upholstery fabric that looks similar to an expensive decorator silk blend.

8. Install drapery rods. When our rods broke in transit, we had to scramble to find a suitable replacement. The faux-finish metal rods we found had attached finials, but the longest rod would extend to only 86 inches, well short of what we needed. We purchased two rods and a saw with a blade that would cut metal. We used the larger-diameter portion of both rods, bridging them with one smaller-diameter portion, minus its finial.

9. Gather the self-lined valance using a running stitch in two places to make three equal swags. (The running stitches mark the spots where the swags wrap around the rod.) After draping the valance over the rod, we hung a panel at each side of the window.

10. Hang the panels at the columns to define the space. We used beaded garlands for the tiebacks. Safety pins hidden in the fabric folds hold the garlands in place.

11. Hang the framed tapestry, and mount the iron sconces on either side. (We "aged" the white sconces by wiping them with a dark bronze acrylic paint and immediately rubbing it off.) We hung a plate above each sconce and placed platters in the sconce arms.

12. Position the sideboard. We then arranged accessories on top. For a more casual look, we leaned the mirror on the sideboard, and, for safety, hung it from a screw in the wall.

13. Lay the rug liner and rug.

14. Place the table and chairs.

15. Add the extras. We sewed runners to the table's dimensions, embellished candles with gold paints and paint pen, and brought seldom-used china out in the open.

16. Get ready for guests. To give the Waldens ideas for setting the table when they host a dinner party, we made place settings from sugared pears, and then added a paper leaf with a guest's name. For the centerpiece, we lined a decorative planter with a plastic trash bag, added floral foam, and then filled the planter with roses and snapdragons. The centerpiece can be swapped out to match the occasion and season. Silk or dried flowers are an option for a longer-lasting bouquet.

here's how

beauty on high

The wallpaper-and-molding treatment on the ceiling above the dining-room table, *page 10,* adds intimacy to the room. To create a similar look, determine the desired size of the design. (The perimeter of the design should be 3–5 inches smaller than the perimeter of the tabletop.) Cut painted molding to the lengths needed to form three graduated-size frames using miter cuts at the corners, tack the pieces to the ceiling, and fill all nail holes. Adhere different wallpaper within each section. Putting the darkest color of paper in the large center area makes the area recede; placing the lightest color in the center makes the room appear more intimate.

custom candles

There's no need to spend a fortune on candles when you can embellish inexpensive ones with paint pens or acrylic paints. The decorators used a simple swirl motif for the tapers on the table. They painted stripes and bands of pattern on the candles for the sconces.

deck the table

The decorators couldn't find reasonably priced table runners in the desired colors, so they made their own. The oversize bottom runner, *page 6,* is made from upholstery fabric that was cut 3 inches narrower than the tabletop and long enough so that it draped over the ends to chair-seat level. Because the fabric is heavy, the decorators finger-pressed (rather than hemmed) the sides. Andee used a zigzag stitch to attach eyelash trim to both ends. If she tires of the look down the road, she can recycle the runner into bench cushions or pillow covers. The reversible top runner combines two fabric remnants on one side and another leftover fabric on the other. (The decorators recommend checking scraps before shopping for new fabric. This saves money and helps coordinate a room by repeating fabrics in different ways. When using small remnants, let the seams become part of the design to avoid the appearance of having run out of fabric in midstream.) Beaded fringe was sewn into the seams of the runner, using a zipper foot on a sewing machine.

before

Refreshing as a sea breeze, this living room is all about casual comfort and livability. Yet it doesn't sacrifice looks or go overboard on seafaring style.

cool calm, & collected

OPPOSITE: A plethora of fabrics gives the window seat, which was in direct view of the front door, a much-needed wake-up call. A plaid valance softens the plantation shutters, and pillows in a mix of colors and patterns turn the formerly underutilized area into a focal point.

Moving into a new house can be a catch-22. Along with all the excitement about new surroundings, there's usually a bit of anxiety about how to decorate. Such was the case when Melinda and Terry Livingstone moved into a three-year-old tract home in Mission Viejo, California. "It was beautiful but bare, and it was just too intimidating for me as to where to start and what to do," Melinda says.

The answers became clear when room decorators Wanda Ventling, Becky Lau Ekstrand, and Robin Tucker stepped in. Where to start? The living room, a much-

used space that's one of the first things visitors see when they cross the front entry. What to do? Infuse it with personality befitting the young couple's casual lifestyle.

The decorators didn't have to go far to find inspiration. The home is located near the ocean, the Livingstones love the water, and Terry is an accomplished surfer. So the team decided to give the blank-slate-of-a-room breezy seaside flair melded with the shabby elegance that Melinda prefers.

Because the home's main level has an open floor plan, with the living room visible from the front door and flowing into other

The room is a blend of styles that is both timeless and unique.

Salvaged stained-glass windows
attached to a wrought-iron display are
an inventive and artful divider in a
cutout between the living room and
front entry. Their weathered look hints
at the shabby elegance of the living
room beyond.

rooms, it put greater demands on the decorating team to ensure that the living room worked within the larger space.

Choosing colors was the first order of business. The decorators wanted to give the room a lively color punch, but they also knew that the palette needed to complement the understated tans and browns of the other rooms. Though Melinda was open to almost anything, Terry was more cautious. He works with new construction, and he didn't care for many of the colors he'd seen splashed on walls. "Please, no Easter-egg colors," he begged.

The outdoorsy palette—blue the color of the sea, sandy beiges, and earthy greens—worked from all angles. The most daring

splash of color is on the walls. Decorative painters applied a wash of aqua glaze over the existing sand-colored walls, using a technique that creates the look of raw silk. The base-coat color peeks through the glaze to echo the color in the other rooms and hint at the beach theme.

Built-in bookcases and a window seat that Terry had previously built received a coat of crisp white paint to meld with the woodwork and plantation shutters on the windows. Though the bookcases and window seat gave the room a charming focal point, they also added to the space's already strong geometric lines due to the wall cutouts, windows, and shutters.

The decorators tackled those issues with fabrics, patterns, and furnishings to soften the room. Durability was their number-one priority with fabrics. Because the room is meant to be lived in, and because the Livingstones have a 19-month-old daughter, the fabrics needed to be able to stand up to daily wear from an active family. Beyond that, the fabrics simply needed to stay within the chosen color scheme and have a casual yet sophisticated look.

Two of the especially whimsical fabrics use animal-like prints in unexpected ways.

OPPOSITE: With a fresh coat of white paint, the bookcases have a clean, crisp look and now seem at one with the moldings. LEFT: In keeping with the room's unfettered feel, the items displayed on the bookcases are simple and simply arranged, with plenty of "white space" around items.

The inspiration for the wash of aqua on the living room walls came from the nearby ocean.

For example, the selections used for some of the pillows include an aqua pinstripe fabric with an animal-print shell motif and a soft green fabric with bold animal-print stripes. Another fabric, an upholstery-weight with chenille puffs, provides great texture.

A large-scale checked print in muted greens, blues, and white is the boldest and most prominently used fabric. Fashioned into window treatments, it breaks up the expanses of solid colors. With kicky box pleats and coordinating piping and banding, the valances look more complicated to make than they actually are. The decorators stapled fabric to a board and added fabric-wrapped cording for a crisp look that's perfectly suited to the room's casual style. "They were so easy to make," Melinda says. "I'm not a seamstress, but I know I could make window coverings like these."

Together, the fabrics—used for cushions, pillows, and window treatments—provide enough diversity of color, texture, and shape to make the room soft and interesting yet with an updated feel.

One of the more surprising choices is the combination sofa/chaise with its white denim slipcover. Although white may seem to be an impractical choice for a family with

a toddler and for a room that gets lots of use, the slipcover removes for washing. It also gives Melinda the option of changing the look if the urge strikes. In the winter, she can substitute a new slipcover in a warmer tone and swap out a few pillows or throws to give the room a new look.

Like the fabrics, furnishings also help tame the room's harsh lines. The 9-foot-long custom sofa spans one wall and offers plenty of cushy comfort. With Terry and Melinda's approval, the decorators selected the 6-foot-long chaise so its rounded end would extend a few inches into the doorway that leads to the front entry, thereby accentuating the curves. The sofa's serpentine front edge further diminishes the living room's strong geometrics.

The room's softer side also is underscored by a chair and ottoman upholstered in a surprisingly durable suedelike fabric that's a gentle shade of lime. "When the chair and ottoman arrived, I knew that this was going to be a very fun room," Melinda says. "I was surprised by the color and the fabric, but I loved them immediately."

Next to the chair, a half-circle console table mimics the shape of the sofa and chaise on the opposite wall. The console was a bargain the decorators couldn't resist. Because it was a damaged floor model, with a deep gouge along the front edge, the price was reduced. The gouged table fit perfectly into the shabby-elegance theme and even needed more distressing. The decorators scraped the edges with scissors and then used a hammer to gently "soften" the scraped areas. To deepen the wood tone, they rubbed black glaze over the table and then sanded off the glaze.

OPPOSITE: Rather than a short-lived bouquet from a floral shop, a blooming plant intended for use outdoors was planted in a decorative bowl and then surrounded with shells. When all the blooms are gone, it can be planted outdoors.

living with color

Nothing sets the tone of a room more than color—a highly personal attribute that draws immediate reactions. Aqua may seem like a daring hue for a living room, but the aqua in the Livingstones' living room is soft and watery, not the vibrant tropical hue that may first come to mind. When teamed with a sage green that borders on taupe, the look is toned down even more.

The lesson learned? Give unexpected colors a try. For example, pink may seem little-girlish, but teamed with a chocolate brown it's all grown-up. And remember that a single color comes in many shades. Reds, for example, run the gamut from bold and intense (think tomato red) to deep and warm (the color of bricks).

When trying a new color, don't be alarmed by how it looks when it's first splashed on the walls. Glazes can tone down the intensity, creating a mottled, chalky effect. Fabrics, furnishings, and accessories all come into play, too.

the room just came together."

One of the room's unique features is the windowlike cutout in the wall facing the entry. Designed to add light and openness to the room, it also makes the living room seem a little *too* open. The cutout itself was stark, but the decorators didn't want to cover it or dress it so much that light wouldn't filter in.

The solution is striking: two salvaged stained-glass windows were transformed into a work of art. An artist created a framework to suspend the windows in the cutout using new and recycled wrought-iron pieces. The piece was designed to be attached with screws to the upper and lower moldings, but the designers decided it needed additional side supports because the Livingstones live in an earthquake-prone area and because it would be in a high-traffic zone.

Another design dilemma Melinda faced was more common: floor-to ceiling bookcases. Shelves are great when books and collections are plentiful, but they can be daunting to homeowners who may not have enough to fill them. Arranging shelves also takes a keen sense of balance and scale—something that fortunately was second nature to the decorating team.

To allow flexibility in arranging the shelves, the decorators purchased more items than they knew they could use and then returned ones that didn't work out. Their shopping list included a few antiques, pottery, translucent glass, and larger items

RIGHT: Melinda and Terry have fun with daughter Lauren in their newly decorated living room. OPPOSITE: The fact that the chaise extends a few inches into the doorway may at first seem like a measuring mistake. It was done on purpose, though, to accentuate the chaise's rounded shape and to soften the room's harsh angles.

such as wicker baskets, bowls that could be filled with moss balls, and covered boxes that double as storage containers. The decorating team's approach taught Melinda a lesson about shelves: It's wise to spend most of your budget on a few items you really love and then fill in the gaps with larger, inexpensive pieces.

With the shelves in order and the biggest work out of the way, the decorators focused on the smaller details that give a room a finished look. The flourishes include organic materials, such as greenery, shells, and a pair of bamboo lamps. To further the shabby-elegance theme, they hung an

impressive grouping of custom-made art above the console table. The art is nothing more than distressed frames and seashells. On the tabletop, bookends made from shelf brackets prop up a trio of books.

At times throughout her room redo, Melinda wasn't sure how things would come together. "As the room transformation took place, my first thought was that I would never have looked at 95 percent of the items the design team chose—not because they weren't beautiful but because of the limits of my imagination," she says. "I would not have thought of putting together the mix of colors, fabrics, and styles the designers chose. As shipments arrived, I thought to myself, 'What are they going to do with this?' I couldn't picture it, although I always knew it would look good."

Melinda gained more than just a pretty and functional living room in the process. She discovered hidden decorating talents. "Now, I think to myself after watching them at work, 'I can do that,'" she says. "At first, when you look at a room, it seems overwhelming. However, when they broke down the process step by step, I could see that it might be manageable.

"Watching them gave me confidence," Melinda continues. "I'm looking at my dining room and I'm feeling courageous enough to tackle a decorating project myself. I've been jotting down ideas and drawing some pictures."

OPPOSITE: Though grouped en masse, the custom-made shell artwork is light and airy so it doesn't overpower the room. The distressed frames were made from molding purchased at a home center. LEFT: A shallow antique bowl in milky white is filled with river rocks, creating a dry garden for low-maintenance hens and chickens. The bowl's graceful design complements the shelf-bracket bookends and weathered frames hanging on the wall.

the decorators' plan

1. Measure the room, including windows, and doors. Draw an accurate floor plan.

2. Measure the furnishings. We were able to use only Lauren Livingstone's little chair because the sofas had been borrowed from Terry Livingstone's mother.

3. Develop a floor plan. Determine what's needed to make the room function well. Because the Livingstones often host friends and family, we knew adequate seating was important.

4. Develop a palette. We considered the home's overall palette when selecting colors for the living room. We also factored in the skin tones of the family members to put them in the best light.

5. Shop for the furnishings and accessories. We allowed extra time for the overall design process because we ordered the sofa/chaise and the fabrics.

6. Empty the room of all furniture and accessories. We also began sewing the pillows, cushions, and window treatments.

7. Apply glaze to the walls.

8. Position the sofa, chair, and ottoman in the room. We also hung the window treatments.

9. Make the shell-theme art. We also found an artist for the window unit.

10. Install the stained-glass window unit in the cutout near the entry.

11. Purchase the remaining accessories and plants. We arranged accessories on the shelves.

12. Add mirrors to two ornate frames and then hang.

13. Age the console table. We scraped and gouged the surface, rubbed it with black glaze, let it dry, and then sanded it off.

14. Arrange the remaining furniture and accessories.

15. Place the window-seat cushion, pillows, and throws.

16. Bring in more plants. We put a blooming plant in a decorative bowl for the coffee table. To further the subtle seaside theme, we covered the soil with rocks and shells. We arranged river rocks around hens and chickens in a shallow antique dish for the side table. Additionally, we planted a large palm in a container and covered the soil with moss.

17. Place additional accessories. We experimented by adding and subtracting items until we were satisfied.

here's how

straight talk

Arranging a grouping of art, such as the seashell frames, *page 25,* is easy when you start on the floor. Tape pieces of kraft paper together to the desired width of the grouping. Lay the paper on the floor, and place the artwork on the paper, repositioning each picture until you have the desired look. Trace around each picture; remove the pictures from the paper. Use painter's tape to tape the paper to the wall. Measure from the top and sides of each picture to where the nail should be, mark the locations on the paper, and nail through the paper, *right.* Remove the paper. Hang the art.

Tip: When attaching the hanging wire to the backs of pictures, cover the areas where it attaches to the frames with a small piece of cardboard or several thicknesses of masking tape to avoid damage to your walls.

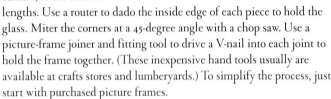

frame it!

The seashell artwork, *right* and *page 25,* is an easy and affordable way to dress up a wall.

To make each distressed frame, use a miter box to cut bead board or molding, available from home centers, to the desired lengths. Use a router to dado the inside edge of each piece to hold the glass. Miter the corners at a 45-degree angle with a chop saw. Use a picture-frame joiner and fitting tool to drive a V-nail into each joint to hold the frame together. (These inexpensive hand tools usually are available at crafts stores and lumberyards.) To simplify the process, just start with purchased picture frames.

Paint the frame with acrylic paint; let dry. Coat the frame with crackle medium, following the manufacturer's instructions. Let dry. Paint over the frame with latex paint. As the paint dries, the crackling process will occur.

Use a file or bristle brush to scrape away small areas, such as in the corners and grooves. Apply a coat of light stain to give the frame an aged appearance.

Have glass cut to fit the frame. Hold the glass in place with framer's points, small finishing nails, or staples. (If you're using staples, position them so they can be bent down to hold the glass in place, rather than imbedding them in the frame.) Staple wire to the back of the frame for hanging.

Use hot glue or permanent long-setting glue to adhere shells and starfish to the front of the glass.

pillow panache

Pillows are the quick-change artists of decorating. Toss them around a room to add instant pizzazz. To simplify the sewing, use square and rectangular pillow forms and choose fun fabrics that are impactful enough without needing trims.

Tip: You can use a variety of tools to create interesting effects on walls. Try old brushes, sponges, crumpled plastic wrap, grocery bags—even a comb. Experiment by painting several pieces of cardboard with the wall color and applying the glaze mixture in different ways.

walls that wow

There's no reason to settle for basic flat walls when it's so easy to add depth, texture, and dimension. The walls in the living room, *page 16,* were painted to resemble raw silk, and the technique didn't involve much more than using a few stiff-bristle brushes and tinted glaze.

To create a similar look, first clean the walls and mask off elements that won't be painted. Use painter's tape, which is easy to remove and doesn't leave marks. If needed, base-coat the walls. (Because the living room walls already were painted a sandy beige, which we wanted as our base coat, we did not need to repaint.)

Tint a water-base glaze according to the manufacturer's instructions; the amount of tinting depends on personal preference. (We tinted our glaze with blue and green paints until we obtained an aqua color that matched the fabrics used in the room.)

Apply the glaze with a stiff-bristle brush that's at least 4 inches wide—the bigger the better. Practice to get a feel for how much glaze to load onto the brush to achieve the desired result. Move the brush over the wall in a continuous top-to-bottom stroke, applying enough pressure to separate the bristles and allow the base-coat color to show through. Work quickly because the glaze dries fast. Allow the glaze to dry.

Use a smaller brush to apply a second coat of glaze; let dry. For more depth and to tone down the walls, use an even smaller brush to apply a small amount of the base-coat paint atop the glaze.

beachy keen

There's no easier way to gain seafaring style than with seashells and starfish, which can be plucked from a beach or purchased inexpensively at crafts stores. Use them as the decorating team did to make artwork, *page 25.* Or, simply layer shells over soil in a potted plant or sit a shell on a book, *below* and *page 20.* The possibilities are endless: Hot-glue small shells to a mirror frame or to picture frames. Thread grosgrain ribbon through a starfish to create a curtain tieback or hanger for a doorknob or cabinet pull. Carefully poke a hole through shells and string them on ribbon to create a garland for a mantel. Or simply fill a glass bowl with shells, tuck in a few photos of a beach vacation, and place the arrangement on a coffee table.

aging gracefully

To achieve a shabby-elegant look comparable to some of the furnishings and accessories in the Livingstones' living room, you don't have to scour antiques stores and flea markets. Wood furnishings and picture frames can be instantly aged by using antiquing or crackling medium or simply by applying a new coat of paint and then rubbing it off before it dries. Use sandpaper or steel wool to roughen wood or metal surfaces in areas that would naturally show the most wear, such as on corners. If you're really daring, use a hammer to add some dings or a paint scraper to reveal older layers of paint.

stylish window wear

The valances, *right, pages 15,* and *page 19*, are a step above the ordinary hang-them-on-a-rod variety. The clean, tailored look comes courtesy of a pelmet board, which is essentially a fabric-draped shelf hung above a window. You can make a pelmet from any type of board, usually 5–7 inches wide. (The decorators used 1×4 boards.)

To determine the length of the pelmet board, measure the width of the window, and add the distance that sheers or draperies will extend at the sides. When the pelmet board is hung, it should cover hardware used for the panels or shades that will hang underneath it. It also should cover the upper window molding. Install L-brackets 1½ inches outside and 4 inches above any curtain-rod brackets.

To determine the pelmet/valance length and width, use these formulas:

- Board length = window width + twice the distance from the edge of the window molding to the end of the valance.
- Valance width = board length + twice the board width.
- Fabric requirements = valance length × valance width (board length + width + allowance for corner pleats) + fabric to wrap the board. (If necessary, piece the fabric to achieve the desired width. If you plan to line the valances, measure and cut the lining the same as for the valance.)

For the complementary border fabric, allow for twice the finished width plus seam allowances along the length and width of the

valance. The border will be finished on the front and underside of the valance.

For the piping at the top of the valance, allow at least 5 inches of width to wrap the cord (purchase thick cord to fit the outer perimeter of the pelmet board plus a few extra inches) and to leave a seam allowance to staple to the pelmet board.

Factor in these tips on fabric: If you use plaid fabric or another fabric with an obvious directional pattern, purchase extra fabric and fit it along the length of the board to determine the position of the center and/or corner pleats before sewing. It may be helpful to make a pattern from kraft paper and fit it to the pelmet board before cutting the fabric. Use interfacing or fusible webbing to give lightweight fabrics added body. Upholstery-weight fabric and cotton-polyester lining will not require additional stiffening.

Use a saw to cut the pelmet board to the desired length. Attach L-brackets to the wall above the window. Position the board on the brackets to check for proper sizing. Mark holes on the pelmet board for the L-bracket screws. Remove the board and drill pilot holes at the marked spots.

With right sides of fabrics together, sew the border strip to the lower edge of the valance fabric. Press the seam allowance toward the border. With right sides together, sew lining along the raw edge of the border. Press the seam toward the lining. Align the top and side edges of the valance fabric and lining (if using), right sides together, folding the border in half. Sew along the sides. Turn

the valance to the right side and press, evenly dividing the border between the front and underside of the valance. Fit the fabric onto the pelmet board, and shape the corner pleats. Staple the valance to the front edge and sides of the pelmet board.

For the piping, cut the accent fabric and the thick cord slightly longer than the finished measurement. Center the cord on the wrong side of the fabric, and fold the fabric over the cord. Sew close to the cord using a zipper foot on a sewing machine. Staple the piping to the edge of the pelmet board along the raw edge of the valance, covering the valance staples, *below left.* Turn the ends of the piping slightly to make a smooth finish where the piping meets the back of the board and the adjacent wall.

To hang the window treatment, use screws to attach the board to the L-brackets.

shelf help

Built-in bookcases offer great display opportunities, but they can present a decorating dilemma. If you don't have a decorator to help out, as the Livingstones did, you can simplify the challenge. To prevent the display from looking like a mishmash, stick to just one color. For example, display ceramic pottery in the same shade of aqua. For a denlike effect, simply fill the shelves with books. If you're short on books, many used bookstores sell boxes of books for less than $15. (Look for books with interesting spines. If they need toning down colorwise, coat the spines with stain and let it dry.) Book jackets can often create a busy look, so consider removing them. Stack some books, and let others stand upright. If you're ready to tackle a more personalized display, have wicker baskets and greenery on hand to fill in gaps.

suite
sophistication

Imagine a private space that is, without apology, a room designed to soothe the weary soul. This six-room master suite is just such a haven. A soft palette and luxurious touches pamper and please.

OPPOSITE: Wispy Roman shades diffuse light above a cushy window seat that spans nearly an entire wall of the master bedroom. LEFT: Positioned on a wall opposite the window seat, the bed ensures that the homeowners awaken to a great view of the outdoors. Rich wood furnishings, including a French bed with cane accents, lend visual weight to the room's soft palette. Bedside lamps with crystal bases and an embroidered silk duvet add elegance. ABOVE LEFT: Overlooking no detail, the decorators took their creativity to the ceiling. A stenciled design encircles a light fixture in the exercise room.

i In pondering a decorating direction for this six-room master suite in a Des Moines, Iowa, showhouse, room decorators Wanda Ventling, Beverly Rivers, and Amanda Reynal had no trouble agreeing: All envisioned an in-home getaway so self-contained, so soothing, and so luxuriously layered in comforts that troubles would dissolve at its door; all envisioned their own fantasy escape.

A meeting with the homeowners solidified the direction. (Unlike many showhouses, this one had occupants. The family would move out during the design process, and then return when the showhouse closed to the public.) The goal was to design an oasis for the busy couple that's apart from the rest of the house—and apart, at least in feel, from their three school-age daughters' bedrooms just down the hall.

Because the master quarters are in a circa-1912 Georgian-style home, the decorating team agreed that the redo should reflect the style and era of the architecture. "We wanted to keep it soothingly understated yet maintain the sense of elegance inherent to the house," Reynal says. Their savvy solution? Bring in traditional antique and reproduction furnishings, rich silks and soft chenilles, and plenty of hand-stenciling and special-effects finishes on the ceilings and walls.

As part of the showhouse, the suite begged for some drama that would wow visitors. Of course, the suite's 1,300-square-foot size was quite impressive on its own. A sumptuous embroidered silk duvet, lush decorative pillows, and a mix of more than 29 fabrics made it even more impressive. But this suite also was grounded in real life. The homeowners had demanding jobs, and their master quarters needed to be a retreat where careers and kids momentarily could take a backseat to sweet serenity.

With that in mind, the decorators selected a soothing, watery palette, starting with a pale blue-green detailed with gold

Quiet colors, rich woods, and sparkly

A mix of patterns gives the bedroom energy. The plaid window dressing draws attention to the window seat. The Moorish stencil on the walls fades in and out, creating an aged look that doesn't compete with the fabrics.

crystal creates a look of hushed elegance.

RIGHT: A double row of trim edges the silk plaid pillow made from the same fabric as the window treatment. OPPOSITE: Eyelash trim adds a playful touch to a shapely rolled-back slipper chair. A Chinese wedding basket on the floor beside the chair and a dowry box on the armoire add exotic flair that subtly permeates the suite.

creating a special space

Even if you don't have a master suite as grand as the one in this showhouse, you can take a few pointers from it. Consider these tips for creating a nurturing at-home retreat:

1. **Choose soothing colors.** Studies show that blues and greens are soothing and calm the mind. Pale neutrals also are contemplative colors, causing worries to vanish.

2. **Indulge in "touch me" softness.** Select feel-good fabrics such as soft chenilles and smooth silks. Toss cushy pillows on chairs and on the bed, and use thickly padded cushions on benches or footstools.

3. **Splurge on luxury.** Even if the budget restricts your extravagance to a single pillow, that pillow will cajole you into a better mood. Similarly, sheets with high thread counts beckon sweet dreams.

4. **Create continuity.** Repeat an element, such as stenciling, velvet-fringe trim, or bamboo accents in your bedroom and bath. You don't want the rooms to seem disjointed and jarring.

5. **Dim the lights.** Provide various lighting options for daytime grooming and nighttime relaxing. Remember: Dimmer switches aren't just for dining rooms. Keep candles on hand, too.

stenciled trellises for the bedroom walls. The pale blues and greens are ideal for lowering the blood pressure, but such a quiet palette easily can become boring, especially with so many rooms. No problem here, thanks to a sprinkling of oxblood reds and burnished coppers "that restores the rooms to life after the muted palette drains it away," Reynal says.

Something else prevented the soothing hues from becoming overkill: The design progresses as you travel from one space to the next, intensifying in both color and decoration. It's also clear which spaces are designed for the woman of the house, which are considered the man's domain, and which are done with both genders in mind.

The journey into the lap of luxury begins by entering the suite from a small vestibule off the landing. The bedroom is to the left, the woman's bath is to the right, and straight ahead, the vestibule opens into a series of rooms that circle back to the bedroom. The dressing room off the vestibule is the quietest, most feminine area. Furnished in French antiques, it has the palest palette, and "just a simple scarf dresses the window," Reynal notes. In the next space—a room-size closet with its own

Creating a calming
environment with
a touch of romance
was the primary goal.

window seat—the palette intensifies with a mid-tone at the ceiling, and the window treatment is a bit more elaborate.

From there, the suite flows into an exercise room via a tuxedo closet. "The crescendo peaks here," Reynal says. Red plays a more prominent role, though still as an accent color, to help stimulate the desire to exercise. The decorators also stepped up the masculine feel by selecting an impressive gentleman's chest topped with trophies and a tortoiseshell-finish box. Still, the elegance continues. "We used silk curtains to make it feel like a room, not a gym," Reynal says.

From the visually pumped exercise room and adjoining gentleman's bath, the suite returns to ultimate calm in the bedroom. Except here, hardwood floors are cushioned with a neutral carpet that visually lightens and physically softens the space. The walls look as though they've been gracefully aging for years. The treatment started with a glaze over a base coat. Stenciling was added later using a Moorish trellis design that fades in and out of view.

The space gets added punch from the apple-green silk plaid draperies. The informal check provides a nice counterpoint to the formal embroidered silk used for the duvet and pillows. A reproduction French cane bed continues the Gallic theme of the dressing room, and bamboo-trimmed furniture and Chinese antiques lend a hint of the exotic to keep the space compelling—just what's needed for a fantasy getaway with all the comforts of home.

OPPOSITE TOP: The French-style dressing room has a soft, aged look. A decorative artist painted the flourishes with custom stencils made to fit the door panels and cabinetry drawer fronts, and then added hand-painted details. The chaise, chair, and marble-top console are French antiques. The chaise was re-covered with cocoa-color velvet and topped with a silk mattress edged with bulky shirred cigar trim. The artwork hanging above it is a framed piece of embroidered silk. OPPOSITE BOTTOM LEFT: A bamboo chair trimmed with eyelash fringe cozies up to a closet window that overlooks the garden. OPPOSITE BOTTOM RIGHT: Crystal knobs add sparkle to the vanity and cabinetry. ABOVE LEFT: In a previous makeover, the homeowners' daughter hand-painted violets on the walls of this bath. The decorating team had a decorative artist add French words and glazing to connect the bath to the suite's overall palette yet keeping the sentimental motifs intact. ABOVE RIGHT: A closet this large calls for special touches. Gauzy sheers are gracefully swooped to the sides of the windows, a radiator is converted into a cushy window seat, and a chandelier hangs above a storage island.

OPPOSITE: A tuxedo closet leads to the exercise room, where a massive chest conveys masculinity. The painted closet's center-panel doors were glazed for a mottled effect. TOP LEFT: A mirrored wall reflects the exercise room and the stenciled ceiling. A pair of bamboo stools is covered in a paisley fabric. The exercise room also can be accessed through the bedroom. TOP RIGHT: This used chest was given a dramatic makeover. It was hand-painted to resemble chinoiserie, in keeping with the Oriental influence that permeates the suite. ABOVE MIDDLE: The simple design painted on the chest top complements the stenciling on the ceiling. ABOVE RIGHT: The chest's original hardware depicts a Native American hunting scene, in stark contrast to the painted chinoiserie design. ABOVE LEFT: The man's bath features English wallpaper and crystal-encrusted sconces. Proving that high style can be attained in ordinary ways, the silk shower curtain was created by adding trim to lined, ready-made draperies purchased at a home center. The insect print came from a hobby store; the bamboo shelving unit that stows towels is an antique.

the decorators' plan

1. Measure the rooms and draw a floor plan. Because this was a six-room suite, the measurements and logistics of placing furniture were crucial. We photocopied the floor plan with the measurements so we had them handy as we shopped for furnishings and fabrics.

2. Meet with the homeowners. We wanted to see what they envisioned. (As it turned out, the the hand-painted flowers on the walls in the woman's bath were off-limits.) The meeting also helped us determine what furnishings to keep and what we need to shop for.

3. Develop a color palette. We chose greens, blues, and creamy whites for their calming effect. Touches of gold, copper, and red energized the palette. We used the colors in different intensities in each room.

4. Assign tasks. We charted out specific responsibilities—sewing, painting, shopping for furniture, and so forth—and scheduled weekly progress meetings.

5. Shop for fabrics. We ended up with nearly 30 different fabrics—and we put each one to good use, especially with pillows. We went wild shopping for trims, too.

6. Empty the rooms of furnishings. We also removed window treatments to create a blank canvas.

7. Paint walls, ceilings, and trim. For continuous flow throughout the six rooms, we limited the walls, woodwork, and ceilings to three neutral cream/beige colors. For subtle differences, we varied the sheens and where the color was used. The cream color used on a wall in one room, for example, ended up on the ceiling of another. For depth, we painted the cabinets in the tuxedo closet a fourth color—a zinc that contrasts with the walls.

8. Add special effects. We went shopping and began sewing pillows and so forth so decorative painters had plenty of space to stencil and hand-paint selected walls, ceilings, cabinets, and furnishings. We installed light fixtures. We added fringes and trims to window treatments, chairs, and pillows.

9. Load the room. We positioned the largest furnishings first. We then set up and dressed the bed. We installed window treatments and the cushions on window seats, and hung the artwork. Finally, after positioning the smaller furnishings, we brought in accessories, including family photos, pillows, throws, and plants. Those little details made the suite sing with style.

10. Take a final tour. The day before the showhouse opened, we made a walk-through to make small last-minute changes, such as plumping pillows and adding fresh flowers.

here's how

stencil savvy

You don't necessarily need custom stencils to get stylish results. The walls in the bedroom, *right, page 31,* and *page 32,* and the ceiling in the exercise room, *page 39,* were dressed up with purchased stencils.

To create a similar look, paint the wall or ceiling in the desired base-coat color. We used a pale cream color. Then we mottled over the surfaces with an equal mix of the cream paint and a slightly darker color to give the walls depth.

Choose the desired stencils. We wanted simple, elegant motifs that had a timeless quality. For the bedroom walls, we also wanted a design that was light and airy. We selected a Moorish trellis-motif stencil.

For a look similar to the bedroom walls, spray the stencil with stencil spray adhesive, and then place the stencil on the wall beginning in one corner. Use a plumb line to keep the stencil pattern vertical. Using a slightly dampened sponge folded in half, pick up a small amount of paint on one end of the fold and dab it into the stencil openings. (If you use too much paint, the paint will run under the stencil edges.) Work on small sections of the wall at a time. Periodically step away from the wall to check the overall pattern.

For a look similar to the ceiling in the exercise room, use acrylic crafts paint to paint a dark black-green border on the ceiling the width of the border stencil. Use the black-green crafts paint and two shades of metallic bronze crafts paint (we used bronze and red-bronze) to stencil a scroll design in the corners of the ceiling. Use a complementary motif to stencil around a light fixture, if you have one that is worthy of extra attention. If you have a ceiling fan, consider stenciling on the wooden blades to bring a style to the center of the ceiling.

Less is more with stenciling. It's easier to add to the design later than it is to correct a busy design. Step away from the surface as you work to judge it from a distance.

dashing details

Think of knobs and pulls as your furniture's jewelry. Adding new hardware is an easy way to add drama to a piece or echo a room's theme. We chose crystal knobs for the cabinetry in the woman's bath, *left* and *page 36,* to add an extra bit of sparkle and underscore the subtle crystal theme used throughout much of the suite. Sometimes, though, you can't beat the original hardware. The refreshed chest of drawers in the exercise room, *page 39,* sports original—and unique—oval hunting-theme pulls. If you plan to update the hardware on an old cabinet or drawer, you'll likely need to fill existing holes and drill new ones because new knobs and pulls often are sized differently. Before you throw out the old hardware, make sure you have a suitable replacement.

artful endeavors

A common mistake people make when hanging artwork is to hang it too high, disconnecting it from the furnishings that surround it and making it seem like it's floating in space. Not so in this suite. The homeowners' great collection of artwork is hung at levels that enable it to become one with the setting. Consider, for example, the two prints that hang above a chair in the bedroom, *right* and *page 33.* The prints are grouped closely together and hang just slightly above the chair; a plant behind the chair visually connects the artwork to the chair. Similarly, the artwork above the bedside tables, *page 31,* is hung just above the tabletops and either even with or just barely above the tops of the lampshades. Being mindful of making artwork a part of the setting also helps ensure that you position it at an ideal height for viewing. Keep in mind that not all art is meant to be viewed while standing. Often, people see it when they're sitting down. So before you get out the hammer and nails, have a seat. Look around the room to determine the height at which the artwork will normally be viewed.

sunny-side up

Invigorating color, cheerful fabrics, new furnishings, and a major decluttering mission lift a neglected sunroom out of the doldrums.

RIGHT: Smart furnishings add order and function to the sunroom. The armoire keeps clutter hidden, the red chair converts into a bed, and the ottoman opens for storage. The narrow table behind the chair doubles as a buffet, and the toile-covered footstool can be used for extra seating.

before

before

Call it the domino effect. The sunroom in Amy and B.J. Leanse's El Paso home had never been much of a showstopper. Amy puzzled long and hard about how to revive the narrow space that had been added on to the house. She had even sought expert advice, to no avail. One company, for example, provided a remodeling bid to the tune of $75,000, which far exceeded what the Leanses wanted to spend.

At their wits' end, family members began to store unwanted furniture and boxes in the sunroom. Eventually, what should have been a cheerful place to relax had morphed into a cluttered storage space. "We just couldn't figure out what to do with it, so it became a junk room," Amy says. "It's embarrassing to say that the crib and stroller belonging to my youngest daughter—she's now 14—were still stored there. That's how little we used it."

Though seldom used, except for retrieving items every now and then, the sunroom wasn't exactly out of sight, out of mind. Both the kitchen and the family room

looked directly into it. The family had to peer through the mess every time they glanced out the windows. The chaos even blocked a great view of the swimming pool beyond the sunroom.

As grim as the situation seemed, the Leanses' problem is common, say the designers who finally came to the rescue. It was a classic case of not having furniture appropriate to the room, thereby minimizing its function and allowing it to become a dumping ground for old furniture and other items. Simply put, the room spiraled out of control because it had never been inviting.

Room decorators Wanda Ventling, Becky Lau Ekstrand, and Holly Craiger looked beyond the clutter and saw a diamond in the rough. Though the room was narrow, it was large enough to allow for some real decorating. The designers knew they could

LEFT: Furnishings positioned on an angle rather than against the walls bring visual relief to the long, narrow space and also define the separate areas. The tile floor was laid on the diagonal to visually widen the room. Valances were kept short to maximize sunlight.

create both seating and dining areas that Amy, B.J., and their daughters would enjoy and be proud of. Amy was ecstatic about the prospect of working with designers who could give the room direction. "I was so excited that I ran screaming through the house," she says.

After scheduling a time for the design team to visit, Amy panicked. "I suddenly saw my room through the camera's eye and felt I had to clean up before anyone saw it," she says. Like a hotel guest who tidies up their room before the cleaning crew arrives, Amy hired a stylist to rearrange the furniture. Then she cleared out enough extra stuff to have a garage sale.

The initial meeting with the designers went well, Amy says. "One of the first things they said to me after looking at the room was, 'We think we can solve your problem.' I was so uplifted by that one comment!"

That meeting took four hours. As the group measured and walked through the entire home to get a feel for Amy's style, they asked lots of questions. The family's lifestyle and Amy's goals for the room were priorities. As they talked, Amy became even

more excited and confident that her downtrodden sunroom would soon spring to life. "They began brainstorming as soon as they entered the house," she recalls. "I was completely impressed with how professional they were and how quickly their thoughts came. They said things like, 'I know exactly what belongs here.'"

Amy, on the other hand, was less decisive. She felt as though she wasn't giving the designers enough guidance. "I really, truly didn't know what I wanted, and my husband and daughters weren't much help," she says. "B.J. wanted an exercise room. The girls wanted a TV room with beanbag furniture. I just joked with them, 'Too bad, guys. I want country French.' The designers asked questions, but I wasn't even sure what my answers should be. They asked if I thought I would sew and do crafts in the room, and I replied that I didn't know. All I knew was that I wanted a room where we could read the paper and drink coffee in the morning."

By the time the designers were ready to call it a day, they had decided that the decor in the kitchen, visible through a big window

in the sunroom, would launch the colors and theme for the makeover. The fruit-pattern wallpaper Amy had hung in the kitchen a few years earlier had the cheerful colors and motifs the designers desired.

With only two weeks to go before the room needed to be photographed, the designers shopped locally for some items, and then caught a plane back to their home base in Iowa to establish a plan and order other items they needed. In the air over Texas, they had a moment of inspiration and designed the window treatments.

Part of Amy's job as a team member was to take inventory of the shipments that began to arrive at her home. The first item to show up was one of the chairs. "I opened up the box, called my mom, and cried, 'It's too good for the room,'" Amy says. Yet she was delighted with each new shipment. "I had always dreamed of having a rack to display plates like the ones I'd seen in catalogs. I opened up one set of plates and then a second set came," she says. "The designers know me even better than I know myself; somehow they managed to find the very things I love."

RIGHT: B.J. and Amy relax with daughters Stephanie, *left,* and Mindy. OPPOSITE: The table is a handy spot for eating, playing games, or doing homework. Scallop-edge seat-back covers and cushions gussy up wicker chairs; the fruit-motif fabric complements the kitchen wallpaper, visible through the window. The decorative folding screen can be moved in front of windows to block the harsh light or provide privacy.

"All I knew was that I wanted a room where we could read the paper and drink coffee in the morning," Amy says.

Casually elegant fabrics and furnishings

LEFT: Small details, such as the piping on pillows and cushions, make a big decorative statement. ABOVE: Fabric-covered boxes scattered throughout the room are handy storage containers and stylish accessories. BELOW: Decorative plates adorn a sliver of wall space above the kitchen window. OPPOSITE: Red-and-white plaid eases the formality of a side chair. Garden touches, such as the wire plant holder filled with greenery, bring the outdoors inside.

Soon, contractors began to show up. (On their initial visit, the designers had arranged for contractors to do much of the heavy work to streamline the process when the team returned.) The style-challenged indoor-outdoor carpet was ripped up and replaced with neutral-color tile similar to that in the kitchen, helping to unite the two spaces. Old doors were replaced with tighter-fitting glass doors that provided a full view of the pool. The old ceiling fans were replaced with new ones that featured elegant frosted-and-clear-glass light fixtures. New moldings were installed to add architectural interest. And to make the space feel more like it was a part of the home rather than an added-on porch, the brick and the paneling were painted the same pale yellow color—an easy and inexpensive way to unite disparate elements.

Having the big tasks finished ensured that when the design team returned a few weeks later, they could focus on the decorative touches that would cozy up the room and make it worthy of daily use. By then, Amy had become accustomed to the swirl of activity taking place all around her.

"I never felt uncomfortable while they worked, partly because the room is away from the rest of the house and we were never inconvenienced in any way, but partly because I felt I knew them right from the start," says Amy, who shares the Midwestern roots of some members of the design team.

Amy delighted in watching the final transformation, which took only two days to complete. The designers "went further than I had anticipated and kept adding extras to my room," she says. The newly painted yellow walls looked just fine to Amy, but the designers went a step further with a dry-brush treatment that gave the walls depth and definition. Furniture that had been shipped was uncrated, and each addition to the room brought it one step closer to becoming a stylish new getaway of which the family could be proud.

"It was so exciting to see the progress," Amy says. "I was amazed at detail after detail the designers added. They kept asking each other, 'Do we have a gap?' If so, they would fill it in. But they didn't overdo it."

The result was near perfection, according to Amy and her family. It's a creative blend of function and style, the casual and the elegant. "And we get to live in it now. I love to just stand and look at it," Amy says. An unexpected bonus for Amy was that the makeover gave the home several hundred more usable square feet. "I don't know how they did it, but now the eye is drawn into this room and out the window, so you get an incredible panoramic feeling. What they accomplished is to extend the kitchen," she says. "Our guests have even commented that they had never noticed our beautiful view before now."

The makeover also helped Amy unearth her preferred design style, something that will serve her well with future decorating projects. Because of all the inherited furniture she had amassed, she'd never truly pinpointed her favorite style. "The designers did that for me," she says. "If this has elements of country French, then this is exactly what I love. I love every single detail. They didn't do too much, and they didn't leave any gaps. We've said 'thank you' a gazillion times."

the decorators' plan

1. Measure the room, windows, and doors. Draw an accurate floor plan.

2. Empty the room.

3. Tear out the carpet and scrape the floor.

4. Lay the new tile floor. We had the tiles placed on the diagonal to visually expand the width of the narrow room.

5. Prime and base-coat the brick and the paneled walls.

6. Prime and paint the ceiling. We used a pale blue with an eggshell finish.

7. Paint all walls the same color to unify the disparate surfaces. We used a creamy yellow paint with an eggshell finish.

8. Dry-brush the walls to add depth. We used paint with an eggshell finish.

9. Paint existing trim. We used white paint with a satin finish. Before installing the new molding, we painted it with the white paint.

10. Install new ceiling fans and lights.

11. Install new doors. We selected glass doors with removable screens. They provide a tighter fit and fuller view. We also caulked windows.

12. Install new molding.

13. Choose fabrics. Drawing on the fruit motif from the kitchen wallpaper, we found a fruit-print fabric and added several others, including a woven grasshopper check and a French toile. We were careful to vary the scales of the patterns—a red-and-white check fabric is the boldest—so they didn't compete with one another or overpower the room.

14. Sew the valances, pillows, bench cushion, tablecloth, chair cushions, and seat-back covers.

15. Embellish the paneled wall with fruit-motif stamps, using the creamy yellow paint with a semigloss finish.

16. Paint the diamond grid on the armoire, and add painted accents to the side table.

17. Clean the floor, windows, and the glass on the doors.

18. Position the rug. We chose a jute rug for its natural look. It anchors the sitting area.

19. Hang the valances.

20. Position the sofa, armoire, bench, and dining table.

21. Place the smaller pieces of furniture in the room.

22. Cover storage boxes with the unused fabrics.

23. Add accessories. For an outdoorsy feel, we added plants, fresh flowers, and twigs in a clear glass vase. A bowl of juicy apples in the room's reds and yellows is another easy finishing touch.

here's how

flying high

Get creative when hanging valances. Drawer knobs in the shapes of dragonflies, butterflies, and ladybugs, *right* and *opposite,* suspend the sunroom valances. Vintage doorknobs are another fun option.

As in most decorating projects, **fabrics were key.** Here, they ran the gamut from casual checks to a formal toile and a perky vintage-inspired fruit print.

extra, extra!

By going a few steps further and adding inexpensive details, the decorators gave the sunroom a custom look.

To enliven the armoire, they used an artist's brush and celery-green acrylic paint to create a carefree, diamond-shape grid on the cabinet door panels, *right* and *page 43.* For a playful element, they glued embossed-metal insect charms, purchased at a crafts store, to the grid in strategic places. (For best results, remove cabinet doors so you can work on a flat surface, and use E6000 adhesive.)

Another little extra was even easier to create. The decorators embellished the dry-brushed paneled walls with rubber stamps in the shapes of apples, pears, and cherries, *right.* They used semigloss paint in the same creamy yellow color used for the base coat on the walls. The stamped images are a subtle but delightful surprise on the formerly lackluster walls.

the power of paint

When choosing paint colors, factor in their mood-altering qualities. With a blue ceiling and yellow walls, there's never a gloomy day in the Leanses' sunroom. Though the colors are soft—especially the blue used on the ceiling—they give the room a cheery, summery feel that lifts the spirits.

reviving a

Soft shades of celadon, rose, and cocoa contrast with the furniture's deep wood tones. An Aubusson-style rug offers comfort underfoot. The chandelier, which replaced a ceiling fan, mixes elegance with whimsy. Plumped with pillows and dressed in cream matelassé with a floral duvet folded at the foot, the bed beckons blissful slumber.

before

classic

A cold-looking and cavernous bedroom in a century-old house gets a warm and cozy makeover. See how creative touches done on a budget can make a big style impact.

"When we wake up, the morning light

h

Homeowners Sara and Jason Broyles thought they had finally found their dream home when they purchased a large 100-year-old Greek Revival house in Davenport, Iowa. Rich hardwood floors, elegant crown molding, deep baseboards, high ceilings, and big windows offered character often lacking in new homes.

What they hadn't bargained for was how the sheer size would stretch their ability to turn the house into a home. Busy raising two children, the young couple hadn't found time to accumulate the quantity of furnishings needed to fill all the rooms. Nor did they have an endless amount of free time to devote to decorating—something that was especially evident in their master bedroom. Though the room was big on features, including a fireplace and separate sitting area, it was short on style.

"There was just so much space and we had so much to do when we bought this house that our bedroom came absolutely last on our list," Sara says.

To the rescue: room decorators Wanda Ventling and Becky Lau Ekstrand. "When I found out they were coming to see it, I went

before

LEFT: The adjoining sitting area is a quiet, sun-drenched nook for homeowners Sara and Jason Broyles. Billowy panels made from the same floral-print fabric as the duvet soften the setting. Three black-and-white photographs mounted on artist's canvases bring contemporary flair to the space. BELOW: Shimmery draperies get extra drama from bands of velvet plissé, fringe, and rose-color lining that peeks out at the top. On the bedside table, a footstool elevates a lamp to the ideal height for nighttime reading.

shining in is just beautiful," Sara says.

through a couple of days when I was a nervous wreck," Sara says. "I just didn't think they were prepared for what they were gong to find, and I was so embarrassed at how parts of it looked."

The design dysfunction began with yellow walls that seemed ill-suited to a space that should be a soothing adult retreat. "It was the worst-looking yellow I've ever seen, but I decided we would just live with it and tackle other projects instead," Sara says. There's more: "We had a tacky fan hanging from the ceiling. For furniture, there was a mattress and box spring on a frame, a couple of dressers, and a computer desk in the room. That was it."

Furniture placement was another issue. This was one of *those* bedrooms that just didn't have a logical place for the bed, due to the windows, doorways, and fireplace that minimized wall space. "We finally put the head of the bed directly beneath a window, which we didn't like at all, but it seemed to be the best we could do," Sara says.

Because of these limitations, the decorating team spent much of its initial visit measuring the room, windows, and furnishings. They also talked to Sara and Jason about their color and style preferences. "You can do anything you want to the room," amiable Jason told the decorators. Sara offered more specific ideas but not so specific that the guidelines would stifle the decorators' creativity.

"We tried not to tell them too much because we didn't want to confuse them with a bunch of ideas that might not work," Sara says. "All I did was look at the fabrics they brought and picked out ones that I liked."

The decorating team left knowing that they wanted to capitalize on the room's best features—its size and the adjoining sitting area. The sitting area offered an opportunity to create a special, cozy getaway for Sara and Jason to relax or read, and the room's size meant that they could make a statement with grand, large-scale furnishings.

Details, such as glistening crystal knobs and flouncy tassels, make the room sing with style.

LEFT: An old cabinet is now a stylish armoire. The floral fabric used for the duvet and sitting-area panels inspired the hand-painted design. OPPOSITE TOP: The fabric used on the tufted folding screen is actually a bedsheet. (Sheets are great options for window treatments, too.) Faux-crystal buttons add a glamorous touch. OPPOSITE BOTTOM: Travertine tile gave the troubled fireplace an updated look. The wall is painted an accent color—pale rose—to draw attention to the fireplace.

To contain costs, the decorators shopped at an outlet store that sells discontinued and damaged furniture. They found the king-size four-poster and two chairs for the sitting area at bargain prices.

In another cost-cutting move, a decorative painter transformed a used cabinet into an elegant armoire. Although the armoire originally was planned to house a television, Sara uses it for storage. "We've discovered that we sleep a lot better without a TV in the room, so we may not ever bring it back in," she says.

To save thousands of dollars in accessorizing the room, the decorators did many of the custom touches themselves. Each project was masterfully handled. One case in point is the draperies. The panels are made mostly from a reasonably priced silk. Then, for a couture look, a more costly velvet plissé fabric was inset in the lower portion. As things go, the draperies ended up being too short, despite the decorators'

diligence at measuring before they began the work. Their savvy solution was to tack on bullion fringe they found at a local store to lengthen the draperies and add a showstopping flourish to the bottom hem.

Another creative solution involved the Broyles' bedside table. With the new—and taller—bed, the nightstand was too short, so the designers simply placed a small footstool atop it to create an elevated platform for a lamp and a nifty compartment for books. The footstool's $30 price tag was a bargain compared to the cost of purchasing a new table.

With the yellow walls gone and a soft color scheme of pale celadon, rose, and cocoa in place, the room is truly restful. Dark wood furnishings add richness. "The other day, I found myself hiding out from the kids to relax in the sitting area," Sara says. "When we wake up, the morning light shining in is just beautiful. We feel so lucky."

RIGHT: Sara and Jason relax in their bedroom with their children Lily, 3, and Austin, 6. The carved traditional-style bed, although not an antique, is well-suited to the century-old home, which is listed on the National Register of Historic Places. OPPOSITE: Small details and inexpensive custom touches make a big impact in the bedroom. *Top row, from left:* Black-and-white photographs "float" on canvas for gallery-style artwork; drapery tops are lined with a contrasting fabric; and faux-crystal buttons add sparkle to an upholstered screen. *Middle row, from left:* Embroidered shades with gentle curves and dangling beads transform a chandelier; new paint and a floral design refresh an old cabinet; and stencils and metallic paint dress up the apron of a table. *Bottom row, from left:* Faux-crystal prisms embellish a purchased window scarf in the sitting area; a band of velvet adds drama to draperies; and silver foil creates striking custom artwork above the fireplace mantel.

the decorators' plan

1. Measure the room, windows, and doors. Draw an accurate floor plan.

2. Measure the pieces of furniture that will stay in the room. We kept one of the nightstands, the matching dresser, and the chest of drawers.

3. Empty the room of furniture. (Sure, this takes some time, but it's always much easier to work in a clutter-free room, especially when painting.)

4. Update the fireplace. We removed the mantel and tore out the tile. We added new travertine tile and reinstalled the mantel.

5. Prepare the walls for painting by filling holes and imperfections. We also sanded the radiators to prepare them.

6. Purchase paint. We used three different, but complementary, colors and varied the sheens for interest. We chose soft colors to create a restful environment.

7. Remove the ceiling fan, and replace it with a crystal chandelier. Embroidered shades on the chandelier are a classy addition.

8. Install window treatments. We hung the fabric panels that separate the sleeping area from the sitting area and added tassel tiebacks to pull the panels out of the way. We sewed faux crystals to the bottom and top edges of an inexpensive ready-made sheer drapery panel to create a scarf for a window in the sitting area. Our crystals came from the lighting department of a home-improvement store.

9. Stamp a leaf motif on the accent wall.

10. Place the rug in the center of the room.

11. Set up the bed frame. We covered the box spring with a fitted bottom sheet. We saved the flat sheet to use as the fabric for the upholstered folding screen.

12. Position the remaining furniture.

13. Create artwork. We painted a stretched artist's canvas in mottled dark brown acrylic paint. We then applied adhesive and silver leaf to form a geometric pattern for the art above the fireplace. We also assembled black-and-white photo canvases to hang on the walls in the sitting area.

14. Make the folding screen. We upholstered it with the unused flat sheet.

15. Stencil the apron of the small square table. We used a silvery cream to create a sophisticated look.

16. Cover the bottom of the firebox with a layer of light-color river rock. We placed an iron candelabra in the firebox atop the rocks, making sure the bottom of the candleholder was securely positioned, and inserted candles that will provide a romantic glow. (Use caution when burning candles.)

17. Add the final touches. We dressed the bed with new linens and pillows, and inserted the homeowners' existing comforter into the floral duvet cover to make a throw for the foot of the bed. We placed a throw and pillows on the chairs, hung artwork, and added crystal lamps and accents. We continued to add and subtract to achieve the desired look.

here's how

artful armoire

Fabrics are great inspiration for pulling a room together. The decorators gleaned ideas for refreshing the armoire from the room's floral fabric, *right.* An artist drew a simplified floral motif that complemented the one on the fabric and then sketched it on tracing paper. Using transfer paper, she retraced the design onto the armoire doors, filled it in with acrylic paint, and added hand-painted details.

silver sensation

Art-challenged individuals needn't throw in the paintbrush. The artwork hanging above the fireplace, *page 56,* requires no special skills yet looks like it was done by a professional. Paint a stretched artist's canvas in mottled shades of brown. Using a wide paintbrush or foam applicator, brush the canvas with leafing adhesive to form slightly irregular sections; let dry. Apply silver leaf, which is available at most large crafts stores, following the manufacturer's instructions.

photo opportunity

It's easy to create gallery-style art similar to the pieces that hang in the sitting area, *page 54.* Enlarge three black-and-white photos (the decorators used flower photos, but you can choose any favorite photos). Trim photos to the same size and then cut three pieces of black foam-core board to the same size as the photos. Use spray adhesive to mount the photos to the foam-core board. Cut three small squares of black foam-core board; hot-glue a square to the back of each mounted photo. Hot-glue each square onto an artist's canvas, available at crafts and art-supply stores. The photos will appear to "float" on the canvas.

screen gem

The upholstered folding screen, *page 56,* is both decorative and functional (it can hide a stationery bicycle, for example). Cover three 6-foot-long 1×6-inch composite boards (sold for shelving) with several layers of quilt batting. Staple each layer on the sides only. Cut a king-size sheet or other fabric horizontally into three equal pieces. Stretch one piece around each board, stapling it on the edges. Trim excess fabric. Connect the panels with piano hinges. Hot-glue flat braid over the edges to cover staples. Mark the placement of buttons down the center of each panel. Staple on each mark. Hot-glue a faux crystal button over each staple.

sheen scene

There's more to paint than choosing colors. Sheen should be factored in, too. To create drama in this bedroom, the decorators used three different paint finishes. The flat paint went on the ceiling—an area that wouldn't need to be washed and that the decorators didn't want to give extra attention. The satin paints used on the walls have just a hint of luster and can be scrubbed. The semigloss paint used on the woodwork and fireplace adds contrast and makes these great features stand out.

With the attic's skylight cleaned and its trim freshly painted, the decorating team applied a deep umber paint to the ceiling to visually lower the roof and give the space an intimate feel.

purely for pleasure

Tucked under the eaves, this elegant attic getaway is a comfy place for watching movies or playing games. Best of all, it's filled with ideas to inspire your own gathering place.

Under the roofline of this 1912 Georgian-style house in the Midwest sits a quiet attic bathed in sunlight and ready to entertain family and friends. With comfy seating, a cozy nook with a game table, and a luxurious powder room, the space transcends the traditional definition of an attic as merely a storage room—or worse, wasted space.

Over the years, this uppermost floor had been redone to become a livable part of the home—a bonus room that could be a child's playroom, a guest retreat, or just about anything else that the homeowners desired. Enter the era

before

ABOVE: To cozy up the stark dormer, walls were covered with a leopard-print wallpaper. Settees upholstered in tiny red-and-white-checked cotton chintz replaced the wraparound bench. (The bench remains above the radiator for extra seating.) The unique pattern combination is easy on the eyes and a bit playful—just like a game area should be. A new pendant light makes the nook usable, day or night.

BELOW: The media area is a study in contrasts. Rich umber walls showcase the aged cream-color finish of the stately entertainment center. Multiple textures—shiny and dull, smooth and rough, soft and hard—add more visual interest. For example, a large shag rug creates an island of comfort on the hardwood floor. The entertainment center graduates to smaller display shelves at the sides, echoing the different heights of the walls.

of the home theater. As part of a showhouse benefitting a local symphony, a decorating team led by Veronica Fisher-Tewell welcomed the opportunity to turn the attic into an elegant media room comprising a theater area for watching movies and a game zone for family fun.

The attic's angled architecture posed the biggest challenge, starting with how to make the sloped walls and ceiling work together. Fisher-Tewell started at the top by painting the ceiling a deep umber to visually lower it. "The ceiling is an important part of a room's design," she says. The same rich color repeats on one wall, but the others are lighter or covered in wallpaper.

In a game area that nestles into a dormer, the architecture is highlighted with a subtle

leopard-pattern wallpaper. Fisher-Tewell took her symmetrical room-arranging cues from the dormer's round window. The window's star motif inspired the design of the custom game table and the half-globe pendant light above it. A pair of matching settees and a bench covering the radiator provide seating around the table.

In the theater area, all eyes turn to the ornate entertainment and display cabinet, which was chosen for details that mimic, the architectural woodwork throughout the house. In front of the entertainment center, two sumptuous pistachio-color chaise longues provide the best seats in the house and cozy up along the sides of a sofa table, creatively positioned to function more like an end table. The chaises are balanced on

The room slowly reveals its playful side: a butterfly on a pillow, monkeys on the wallpaper, and a lamp with a tutu-clad frog.

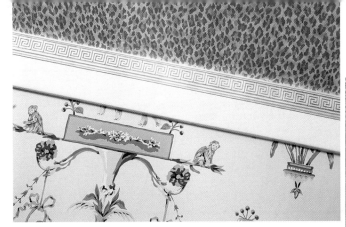

the other side of the room by a two-cushion sofa that helps form a luxurious corner "box-seat" viewing gallery.

When intermission hits, every good theater provides a place to freshen up. Just down the hallway, Fisher-Tewell pulled together a stunning powder room. She repeated the game area's leopard-print wallpaper, installing it on the powder-room ceiling. Then for a change of pace, she covered the walls with a fanciful floral print.

A pedestal sink with curved iron legs and frosted-glass edges, that seem to drape like fabric, serves as sculpture in the powder room. "Once the washbasin was installed, the rest was easy," Fisher-Tewell says. And that's just as it should be in an attic space that's designed purely for pleasure.

OPPOSITE: The lushly decorated powder room features a curved French bench that complements the sink base, towels adorned with detachable fringe, and a classic urn. LEFT: Spray-painted lacquer black and outfitted with glass doorknobs, a chest of drawers commands attention. ABOVE LEFT: A strip of carved molding installed above the existing trim provides extra definition between the wallpapers. ABOVE RIGHT: Beaded pendants are stylish general lighting.

the decorators' plan

1. **Measure the rooms.** With the dormer in the main room and sloped walls throughout, precise measurements were crucial to ensuring that we purchased the right furnishings and accessories. We measured the doorway and stairway, too. Getting big pieces up the steps of a converted attic can be tricky.

2. **Meet with the homeowners.** Because this showhouse was occupied, we sought input from the homeowners. We wanted to find out the room's primary function. We also wanted an idea of the number of people who would be in the room at any one time to determine appropriate seating.

3. **Choose colors.** Because the space will be used by adults and children, we wanted a sophisticated yet casual look. Creams and umber set a relaxing tone.

4. **Select paint and wallpapers.** We chose a leopard-print wallpaper that complements the umber and cream paints. The motif is fun for kids and adults. The wallpaper for the powder room has a floral-and-monkey motif.

5. **Empty the room.** Though the space seemed larger with the furnishings moved out, we knew it would fill up fast, especially with those angled walls.

6. **Update the wiring.** We hired technicians and electricians to upgrade cables and wiring for the TV, stereo equipment, and overhead lighting.

7. **Shop for and order furnishings and accessories.** Comfort is key in this room, so we made sure we test-drove chaises, sofas, and settees before making any purchases. Fun accessories, such as the magic-theme poster, energize the room.

8. **Paint and wallpaper the ceilings and walls.**

9. **Install light fixtures and the bathroom sink and mirror.** For drama, we chose artsy items, not conventional ones. This was especially important in the size-challenged powder room. The pedestal sink is almost like a sculpture.

10. **Place rug in the theater area.** The shaglike rug we added softens the hardwood floor and anchors the seating.

11. **Bring in the furnishings.** We allowed extra time (and help) for getting the big items up the stairs.

12. **Hang artwork and accessorize.** After everything was in place, we popped in a movie and took a seat to make sure there was a good view from every angle.

here's how

2

set the stage

Lights! Camera! Action! Move your media room—or any room, for that matter—front and center with these design tips:

1. Display for drama. Open shelves are the perfect stage for displaying family treasures, photos, and collectibles. For greatest impact, vary the sizes, shapes, textures, and subject matter of displayed items.

2. Light the set. Match the desired mood with appropriate lighting. This media room has a mix of general and task lighting. Funky Parisian chandeliers add dramatic detail, with beaded shades and a crystal swag. A wireless lighting-control system allows lights to be dimmed during viewing.

3. Throw in an unexpected plot twist. A grouping of six framed red antique ceiling tiles creates dramatic wall art. Choose interesting materials and showcase them in fresh ways.

4. Add the props. Provide pillows and floor cushions in feel-good and look-great harlequin, floral, and leopard-print fabrics. Add dazzle with beads and eyelash and feather trims.

4

3

before

WOW! Every teen dreams of a bedroom that elicits rave reviews. Revved up and raring to please the younger crowd, this retreat is now the coolest hang-out on the block.

bring on the color

When room decorators Kristin Schmitt, David Anger, and Traci Baldus revamped this suite as part of a Midwestern showhouse, they let the fashion fancies and energy level of its teen resident inspire them. Although the suite is designed for a youth, it's popping with ideas for all ages. Turn the page to see how they energized the three-room suite.

wow 'em with a
wake-up call

Color and pattern rule in the suite's lead-in bedroom *above* and *opposite,* but also check out the elements that make it live as great as it looks. vivid and visual To kick-start the redo, the decorating team chose a dynamic palette and proved that citrus orange, hot pink, and zesty green can play well together. Every room is rooted in green, with the other colors splashing about. Patterns are plentiful and in sync thanks to their geometric nature. earning her stripes Look closely: The walls' whimsically imperfect stripes are really wallpaper. The generous-size room welcomes the large pattern, and wallpaper is a labor-smart alternative to hand-painting a design. (If you haven't shopped for wallpaper lately, you'll be surprised by the fun designs.) sleek storage Teens want a look that's radical, but they need a space that functions well, too. Rather than a predictable (and boring) bookcase, the designers hung an artistic arrangement of wooden cubes on a wall adjacent to the bed. The backs are painted in contrasting bold colors. crisp and clean A tailored classic, Roman shades dress the windows while showcasing favorite fabrics. The style is easy to line, too, for room-darkening privacy. Clean-lined furnishings, some with retro-inspired curves, veer the room to the mod side.

The simple concept of a dressing table became a sleek design element when the decorators joined two matching lingerie chests with a wood-framed laminate top. A cool mirror and stool added funk.

practicalities can become fun and sassy.

before

pour on the
creativity

The bedroom's French doors open to a sun-drenched room. The decorators transformed the room into a combination sitting area with kick-back seating, *opposite,* and an art studio, *above,* with plenty of work space and walls that are a work-in-progress canvas. in transition Staying true to the bedroom's scheme but steering clear of matchy-matchy, the decorators doused the room's limited wall space in solid green rather than using the striped wallpaper. The multicolor-checked fabric makes another play, but a new square motif is introduced through subtler sheers. less is more With lined shades on the French doors offering privacy, the decorating team could simply frame the fabulous windowed walls with graphic curtain panels. Vertical stripes of opaque green linen hang behind geometric-printed sheers in each corner. magnetic attraction Magnetic paint simulates bulletin boards over the drawing table and on the neighboring wall—perfect for displaying sketches, today's Hollywood hottie, and photo memories.

darling, you look marvelous

The suite's small adjoining bath had fallen by the wayside, mired in a past era. Continuing the lively scheme was just the pick-me-up it needed. With a crisp new white "canvas" and the addition of colorful accessories, *opposite* and *above*, the bath now makes a real splash. good as new Initially, dark, dingy, out-of-date tiles dominated the bath's walls and floor. Plus, drab gray was the fixture color of choice. The decorators skipped a major remodeling headache by having the wall tiles and bathtub resurfaced with a permanent acrylic-resin finish. They swapped in a stylish new sink and toilet and covered the existing floor tile to breathe new life into the room. seeing circles Bold color and graphic shapes stayed in the game, but the decorators threw the small space a curve with circles galore. The whimsical wallpaper choice starts the room in the green, of course, and more subtle circles repeat across the shower curtain. Stripes strike the pattern finale. outdoor favors Products designed for outdoor use are the shining stars of this moist environment. Fabric with a water-resistant coating fashions the shower curtain and roller shade, and a sheet of woven vinyl covers the old tile floor.

before

the decorators' plan

1. Measure the rooms, and draw an accurate floor plan.

2. Meet with the teen. We wanted to get a feel for her personality and needs. (Remember: Kids have great ideas that can be incorporated into a room, so let them be a part of the process.) We checked out the teen's closet, too, to get a sense of her style.

3. Factor in function. With schoolbooks, CDs, and toys, a young person's room has storage needs beyond just clothing. Because our teen is artistic, we also wanted to give her a studio area to get her creative juices flowing.

4. Choose the colors. Younger people are more open to wild colors, so we had fun choosing vibrant hues for this room. After we chose our palette, we began shopping for fabrics, furnishings, and accessories.

5. Empty the rooms of furniture. We also removed the window treatments.

6. Oversee the contractors' work in the bathroom. We checked the progress at the end of each day to ensure it was done to our specifications and prevent any last-minute surprises.

7. Start sewing. We softened the room with a duvet, pillows, cushions, and window dressings. Floor cushions are great for teens, so we made plenty to toss around.

8. Paint the walls. We also hung wallpaper in the bedroom, closet, and bathroom.

9. Create the dressing table. We installed the laminate top, and then brought in the matching chests and hung the mirror.

10. Create the shelving unit. We laid the shelving cubes on the floor to determine the desired arrangement, based on the wall measurements. We then painted the backs of each cube in different colors to make the unit pop.

11. Install the shelving cubes, window treatments, mirrors, shower curtain, and towel bars.

12. Place large furnishings in the rooms. We then set up the bed and dressed it. Next, we positioned the smaller furnishings.

13. Add the accessories. We had lots of fun with this suite. For example, we used bottles of colorful nail polish and little chairs that hold jewelry as inexpensive accents on the dressing table.

here's how

seven steps to style

This teen suite is so chock-full of ideas, it's hard to notice everything on a first tour. Here's a recap (and a few ideas we haven't mentioned), along with tips to guide your next room makeover:

1. **be color-confident.** The decorators stuck to their color game in each room. They had great fun mixing textured fabrics and playful trims.

2. **repeat yourself.** When done right, repetition isn't boring. The contrasting binding on the Roman shades subtly echoes the duvet cover, *page 74,* and shower curtain, *page 81.*

3. **leave nothing undone.** With wallpaper, fresh trim paint, and wiggly handles on the built-in drawers, it's OK to peek into this closet.

4. **nix conventional thinking.** Curtain cable systems are a sleek alternative to traditional rods. Typically mounted to the wall, these were moved up to the studio's ceiling.

5. **get creative with paint.** The magnetic paint on the studio walls is a gray base coat applied wherever a magnetic surface is desired. Once it's dry, just paint over it in the desired color or colors.

6. **find savvy storage solutions.** Constructed from maple, custom shelves meet both storage and display needs.

7. **be adventurous.** The bath's sisal-like woven vinyl flooring was designed for outdoor use, but it works beautifully indoors (and it was easy to install).

New French doors on both sides of the room shut out noise yet keep the space from feeling closed in. Roll-up shades lower for privacy.

before

all in a
day's
work

Captain David Zacharias has confidently sailed the seas as a career officer in the U.S. Navy, yet when it came time to retire and drop anchor in a permanent port, he and his wife, Dana, were stymied.

They planned to convert the seldom-used living room in their Virginia Beach, Virginia, home into an office to accommodate David's future endeavors, which included completing his master's degree and starting a consulting business. However, the space had become little more than a makeshift dining room with cluttered bookcases, and transforming it into a functional office that integrated with the rest of the home was a daunting task, indeed.

"The office is the first room visitors see off the foyer, so we wanted it to be presentable as well as functional," Dana says.

"The furniture we had accumulated was old, from at least two duty stations ago," Dana says. "It wasn't in good enough shape to have out in the open and have people view as they enter our home. The office is the first room visitors see off the foyer, so we wanted it to be presentable as well as functional."

Dana and David's dilemma is common in this computer-driven age. More and more homeowners are converting formal living rooms, guest bedrooms, and other seldom-used areas into home offices—often with no plan as to how to make the reconfigured space both stylish and functional.

Wanting to give her husband the best military retirement gift possible, Dana sought the help of room decorators Wanda Ventling and Becky Lau Ekstrand. Design plans were completed through a whirlwind of e-mail messages and phone conversations, with the Zacharias family providing a videotape and measurements of the room.

LEFT: A painted zebra-stripe floorcloth gives the room a graphic jolt. A wicker suitcase raises the leather-base lamp to the perfect reading height, and a folding chair doubles as artwork on the wall.

The military roots of British Colonial style made this a natural choice for David's home office.

The strategic plan: Develop a British Colonial look that would work with the rest of the home. The military roots of British Colonial style made this a natural choice for the home office.

With a plan in hand, David and Dana oversaw the work of electricians and technicians who upgraded wiring and lighting and installed computer cables and phone lines. A wallpapering team hung a linen-color grass cloth on three walls and a cocoa-color paper on another. Workers hung French doors in the open doorways that led to the dining room on one side of the office and to the front entry on the other.

Meanwhile, back in their own office, the decorating team tracked down furnishings, window coverings, and accessories to create a casual elegant look. The idea was to play dark woods off light walls. The cream-color wallpaper and the twill fabric they found for the shades would provide just the right contrast for the rich wood tones and textural mix of reed and bamboo accents. They also

LEFT: The leather chair and ottoman are dressy enough to impress business acquaintances yet comfortable enough for relaxing. Every detail—right down to the pillows on the chair—was chosen to further the British Colonial look.
ABOVE: David and Dana, with children Darin, *left,* and Devon, gather in their favorite sitting spot.

"I learned that preparation is 90 percent of the work," David says. "Get the electrical and computer cables installed first, so the decorating can follow."

before

ABOVE: The living room, looking toward the entry hall, served most recently as the family's dining room.

made sure that their choices would complement the decor in the rest of the home, which already had many furnishings and accessories in warm wood tones, bamboo, wicker, and leather.

Because the makeover room needed to function first and foremost as an office, the decorators weren't shy about bringing in office furniture. A shelving and storage unit spans an entire wall, providing a combination of display space, drawers, and hidden storage for a computer printer and other equipment. A desk was positioned perpendicular to a section of the unit, extending into the room to create a peninsula-style work space and giving David a view out one set of French doors, rather than of a wall. The creative desk placement also opened up space for chairs for clients. Two bookcases that the homeowners owned flank the picture window for more storage.

The furnishings are flexible, too. Because the desk is a freestanding unit, it can be moved to another position if David needs a change in outlook. The lower and upper portions of the shelving unit separate and can be used in different configurations.

Having lost their formal living room, the couple hoped for a space that could do double duty as a conversation area. The

decorators delivered on that goal, too. They incorporated seating for six, starting with a tufted-back, nailhead-trimmed leather chair and ottoman and armchairs with woven down-filled cushions. Then they creatively expanded the seating options with bamboo folding chairs decoratively hung on the walls, out of the traffic flow. The chairs can be pulled down and opened in a moment. Dana knew the office could be a perfect male-bonding spot for David and his friends. Of course, it's not too masculine to be off-putting to Dana's friends, too.

The function doesn't end with the flexible furnishings. To ensure that the room would look shipshape even if unexpected guests dropped by and clutter was a bit out of control, David or Dana can simply lower the roll-up canvas shades the decorators hung on the bookcases and French doors. This solution is one of David's favorite features. "Our bookshelves always looked cluttered," he says. "The covers are such a clever and yet simple way to hide the mess." And, the shades on the doors allow privacy when David is deep in study. "With two daughters, I can close the doors to 'peeping Sallies' and retain my privacy."

Another creative touch is the wallpaper. The decorators chose the cream-color paper for three walls to provide contrast to the room's dark wood furniture. Then, the wall with the shelving unit was covered in a cocoa-color wallpaper so the shelving unit would recede into the wall and give the illusion of built-in cabinetry.

LEFT: The decorating team's creativity shows in numerous ways. From *top,* a corkboard made from woven cork strips and pushpins made from metal buttons add style; cloth napkins and place mats are fashioned into pillows; a painted floorcloth adds pizzazz; and shades that roll down over two bookcases tie in place for a tidy look.

Because the room has a large picture window facing the street, window treatments with a privacy feature were necessary, especially because the room would be used at night. The decorators chose coverings featuring a two-tone bamboo look; micro-pleated shades behind the woven woods can be raised or lowered independently for privacy and light control.

Accessories also were chosen for their ability to further the British Colonial theme. Wood and leather lamps, a painted zebra-stripe floorcloth, nautical-theme items, and a trunk made by a fellow sailor are welcome additions. David and Dana's favorite item, though, is the palm-frond ceiling fan. "It reminds us so much of our adventures in Singapore and the Long Bar in the historic Raffles Hotel there," Dana says. "I flew in to meet David when his ship anchored in port during a six-month deployment, and it was a really special time and place for us."

Though the room is no longer a living room per se, it's a room that gets plenty of living. Dana often can be found nestled with a book in the cushy leather chair, while diligent David gets down to business at his desk. With its rich and inviting feel, the office has become a place for both of them to retire—contentedly and confidently—from the rest of the world.

the decorators' plan

1. **Measure the room** and discuss requirements for its new functions, including seating, lighting, storage, and work space.

2. **Draw a floor plan.** We also researched furniture options and ordered new furniture, wallpaper, doors, and window coverings.

3. **Run electrical wiring** to the center of the ceiling; install the ceiling fan. We also had workers install electrical and phone lines and computer cables in the work area.

4. **Hang the wallpaper.** We hung the darker color behind the wall unit so the unit would blend with the wall.

5. **Install French doors and molding.** We stained and varnished the items before installing them.

6. **Uncrate the wall unit.** After we placed it in the room, we had a better sense of scale.

7. **Position the homeowners' bookcases.** We put one bookcase on each side of the picture window. To hide clutter, we installed a canvas roll-up shade, and attached hook-and-loop-tape tab-ties, on each bookcase.

8. **Lay the sisal-look rug.** We also made a zebra-stripe floorcloth and positioned it.

9. **Position more furnishings.** We brought in the desk and chair first, and then the leather chair and ottoman.

10. **Install the window treatments** on the picture window. Bring in chairs.

11. **Hang the two folding chairs.** We also arranged accessories and the lamp on the table by the picture window.

12. **Organize the shelves** on the wall unit and the bookcases.

13. **Make no-sew pillows.** To simplify the process, we used cloth napkins and place mats.

14. **Construct the corkboard.** We hung it on the wall behind the desk.

15. **Hang the canvas roll-up shades** on the French doors.

16. **Create custom paper goods.** We embellished plain file folders with road maps and stamped paper to make stationery to leave as a gift for the homeowners. We also stocked the desk and cabinets with office essentials so the homeowners could immediately put their new office to use.

here's how

history lesson

What's the origin of British Colonial style? When traveling the world, British officers took along items that reminded them of the comforts of home. These pieces of finery, mixed with newfound souvenirs, were set amid a backdrop of canvas tent flaps, worn leather, and well-traveled trunks. The result is a military-orderly design style that mixes refinement with ruggedness.

building a better office

There are home offices with computers sitting on tables and uncomfortable kitchen chairs pulled up. And then there are home offices that really function. David and Dana Zacharias' home office falls squarely into the latter category.

The room's function starts with good lighting. Formerly lacking overhead lighting, the room now has a palm-frond ceiling fan outfitted with light fixtures for stylish general lighting. Task lighting, including the floor lamp, *left* and *page 88,* is equally fashionable. The large shelving unit has built-in under-shelf lighting to showcase displayed items, and a brass desk lamp lights up David's primary work space. To deal with another lighting issue—computer glare—shades on the windows and French doors can be lowered.

Comfortable chairs are another home-office must-have. The leather desk chair offers enough support for long hours at the computer, and the two down-cushioned chairs in front of the picture window provide plenty of seat depth and width to make clients feel comfortable. The leather armchair and ottoman are pleasurable indulgences. Two bamboo folding chairs hung on the wall take the place of expensive artwork and can be pulled into service for larger groups.

Order is important in every office—especially when the room is visible from the front door, as it is in the Zacharias' home. The cabinetry and freestanding desk offer hidden storage. The modular wall unit's flexibility is a bonus for a converted room; it can be moved and reconfigured if the family decides to reclaim the space as a living room or if they move to a different house.

a sea of calm

Two grass-cloth wallpapers, *below left* and *below middle,* create a soothing backdrop for this home office. The cream and cocoa colors are neutral enough that they could still work if the room's function changes down the road. Their texture works well with the bamboo and wicker chairs, leather lamp, and sisal-look rug. The herringbone twill fabric, *below right,* is the perfect weight and pattern for the tent-inspired roll-up shades on the bookcases and French doors.

paper goods

Having stylish office supplies may just be incentive enough to tidy up or pen a note. Old road maps dress up file folders and a rubber stamp turns plain paper into custom stationery, *above.*

fancy floorcloth

Animal prints work well in many styles and types of rooms, and their bold pattern makes a big impact. (Use them sparingly, though, to keep from overpowering a space.) The rug, *page 86*, mimics a real zebra skin but actually is made from artist's canvas.

To create a similar rug, tape together kraft paper to make a piece of paper large enough to draw a template for the desired rug size. Using a pencil and the photo on *page 86* as a guide, draw a freehand zebra-skin shape on the paper. Use scissors to cut out the template.

Tape the template to preprimed artist's canvas, available at art-supply stores. (We used about 2¼ yards of canvas.) If preprimed canvas is not available, prime an artist's canvas with gesso; let dry. Use a pencil to trace around the template onto the canvas, allowing at least 3 inches for hemming the floorcloth. Cut out the shape 2½ to 3 inches beyond the traced line. Turn the canvas facedown. Turn the raw edges to the back, clipping and notching along curves as needed. Use a rolling pin to press the edges flat. Seal the edges with double-stick carpet tape for a clean finish.

Using the photos on *page 86* and *above* as references, use a pencil to draw a long center stripe and side stripes onto the canvas. Keep the stripes uneven for a natural look. Use a 1-inch-wide flat brush and black acrylic exterior flat latex paint to paint the stripes. Apply as many coats of paint as necessary to achieve an opaque look, letting the paint dry between coats.

Dilute one part taupe acrylic crafts paint with one part water. Working on a small area of the rug at a time and overlapping adjacent painted areas, brush on the diluted paint. While the paint is wet, wipe off most of it with a dry cloth. Let the paint dry. Use more of the diluted taupe paint and a spatter brush to randomly spatter paint onto the rug; let dry.

Dry-brush undiluted taupe paint onto the rug, covering a small area at a time. To dry-brush, dip a brush into a small amount of paint, dab off most of the paint onto a paper towel, and use short brushstrokes to lightly and randomly brush color onto the rug. Let the paint dry.

Apply a coat of satin-finish water-base polyurethane to protect the painted design. Let dry. Following the manufacturer's directions, apply paste wax to the rug. Allow the wax to stand for 15 minutes and then polish with a soft, dry cloth.

To maintain the rug, wipe occasionally with a damp cloth to remove soil and then wipe with a dry cloth. Rewax as needed.

made in the shade

The decorators made quick work out of installing the roll-up canvas shades on the French doors and bookcases. Their secret weapon? Adhesive-backed hook-and-loop tape. The process didn't involve much more than applying a strip of the tape to a shade and then peeling off the protective paper strip and adhering the tape to the door or bookcase. When rolled down, the shades on the bookcases neatly secure in place with ties, also attached with the same hook-and-loop tape. The tape is also an easy way to adhere a skirt to a dressing table or pedestal sink.

no-sew pillows

No one would ever guess that the decorative pillows, *page 88,* are simple no-sew varieties that, in a previous life, were place mats and cloth napkins. For a dressy look, choose place mats and napkins with woven or sewn-on trims. Use iron-on fusible webbing for hems and seams. A pillow form will be needed for each pillow cover; allow for flanged edges.

■ **Postcard-motif pillow:** Refer to the front pillow, *page 88,* to plan a design using two rectangular place mats and an aged postcard, envelope, or photo. Copy the postcard or other item onto iron-on photo-transfer paper. Most photocopy stores will do this for a minimal charge. Following the manufacturer's directions, transfer the image onto the center of a place mat; let cool.

On the back of one place mat, press iron-on seam tape along three edges. With the back sides of the place mats together, press to bond. The tape will create a narrow flange. Insert a pillow form. Place iron-on seam tape along the open edge; press to bond.

■ **Nautical-inspired pillow:** Refer to the striped pillow with cording, *page 88* and *page 91.* Layer two striped napkins, back sides together. About 1¼ inches from the edges, mark the placement for a grommet at each corner and at three equally spaced points along each side. Use a grommet tool to insert grommets through both napkin layers on three sides. Insert a pillow form. Add grommets to the fourth side. Lace midweight cording through the grommets, leaving 10 inches of cording at each end.

For a nautical finish, tightly wrap about 2 inches of each cording end with duct tape or masking tape. For each end, cut a length of white cotton twine at least 36 inches long. Loop one end and hold it parallel to a wrapped rope end, with the loop extending ½ inch beyond the wrapped end and the short end of the twine extending 2 inches from the wrapped length. Beginning where the tape and rope meet, tightly wrap the long end of the twine around the tape. At the end of the wrapped rope, insert the twine through the loop. Hold both loose ends of the twine; pull until snug. Release the longer end, and continue pulling the other end to bring the loop inside the wrapping to about the midpoint, securing the wrapping. Clip the ends of the twine close to the wrap. Repeat for the other rope end.

■ **Stamped photo pillow:** Refer to the pillow on the left side of the chair, *page 88.* Using a rubber stamp with ink, randomly stamp two cream-color napkins that have decorative edges; let dry. (We used a stamp with the words to the Pledge of Allegiance, *below,* and gray ink.) Use a press cloth and a dry iron to heat-set the ink. Photocopy an old photo onto iron-on photo-transfer paper. Following the manufacturer's instructions, transfer the image onto one napkin, *bottom.* Press iron-on seam tape along three sides of the back of a stamped napkin. Align the two napkins, with back sides together. Press to bond the three edges. Insert a pillow form, creating a narrow flange. Place iron-on seam tape along the open edge; press to bond.

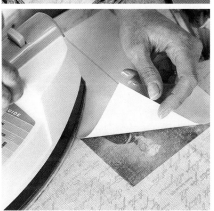

woven wonder

Every office can use a corkboard to hang mementos and important reminders. Woven cork strips create the unique look for the corkboard, *page 84* and *page 91.*

Place corkboard, which is available by the roll at most art stores and home centers, on a flat surface. Place heavy books atop the corkboard for several hours to flatten it.

Remove the backing from a picture frame, or cut foam-core board to the size of the frame to make a new backing. Remove glass, if present; the glass will not be needed for this project.

Measure the length and width of the backing. Add 2 inches to each measurement to determine the length of the cork strips, allowing for weaving. Use a yardstick and painter's tape to measure and tape off 2-inch-wide strips to the determined

lengths. Use a crafts knife or scissors to cut the strips. To minimize measuring, place lengths of 2-inch-wide low-tack painter's tape side by side, and cut between them.

Lay the backing on a flat work surface. Lightly tape it in place across the corners. Beginning at the center and working outward, lay cork strips vertically across the backing, extending the strips beyond the backing. Do not adhere the strips to the backing at this point. Check to ensure that the strips are aligned and straight. Tape the upper ends of the strips to the work surface. Weave the remaining cork strips horizontally through the vertical strips, keeping the strips snug and even. Where necessary to prevent buckling, apply a small amount of hot glue between the strips as you weave, *above left.*

After weaving, lay heavy books atop the strips for several hours to further flatten them, if desired.

Trim the ends of the cork strips even with the backing or foam-core board. Adhere the woven cork to the backing with hot glue or rubber cement, applying it liberally around the edges and conservatively near the center. Insert the backed woven cork into the picture frame. Secure with picture-frame brads or glue.

custom pushpins

These corkboard pushpins are cute as a button—and, in fact, are part button. The decorators used nautical-theme metal buttons, but you can choose a motif that fits your decor. Use wire cutters or heavy-duty scissors to remove the shanks from metal buttons, *below left.* Press flat-head tacks into leftover pieces of foam-core board used for the corkboard or into plastic foam for support. Apply a small amount of heavy-duty bonding glue to the back of each button, *below right,* and to the head of each tack. Press the button and tack together; let dry.

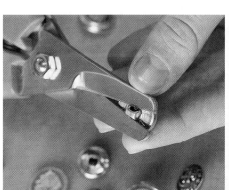

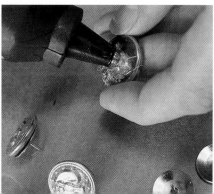

decorating lessons

Let's face it:

Few people have the luxury of a sky's-the-limit decorating budget. There's no need to fret, though. In the end, it's not how much money you spend on decorating that matters but how wisely you spend it. Imagination is your biggest ally. These tips will help guide you to a room of your dreams that is also within your means:

Try some quick changes.
Simply rearranging the furniture—floating it away from the walls or turning it on the diagonal—can transform a tired room. So, too, can moving a piece of furniture or art from one room to another. Remember to experiment to make the most of what you have before you shop for replacements.

Paint it pretty.
Nothing transforms a room more than paint, be it on walls, floors, or furnishings. If you're a play-it-safe-with-white-walls type, you might be surprised to learn that white intensifies the perception that something is missing from a room. It also produces a gallery effect that almost demands beautiful objects and furnishings. Pastels and darker hues have a way of filling up a room's blank spaces and taking the focus off furnishings.

Size things up.
Scale is as important to a room as color and fabrics; it gives a room a sense of proportion and balance. Sometimes, it's obvious when an item is too large or small for a space. Often, though, determining scale takes a keen eye and a lot of practice. A common mistake is to use things that are too small for a space. To break the habit, it's generally best to have at least one worthy focal-point element that commands attention. Try an oversize mirror instead of several small ones, for instance. Consider a large armoire instead of four tiny tables. Six small throw pillows won't do as much for an ordinary sofa as two 24×24-inch ones, which can change the sofa's profile and personality dramatically.

Be art-smart.
Even if you can't afford a masterpiece, you don't have to settle for bare walls. Pages from a book of botanical illustrations or architectural sketches can be cut out, matted, and framed. An ordinary print or poster can turn into an extraordinary piece of art by splurging on professional matting and an elaborate frame. Experiment with positioning, too. Three framed prints butted up to one another can give the illusion of one larger—and more impressive—print. And think beyond framed pieces. A section from an old iron gate or a folded-up bamboo chair can become stylish wall art, too.

Create windows that wow.
For many homeowners, windows are the most challenging part of decorating a room. To get started, factor in the room's function. If you need privacy, for example, you know you'll need a shade, blind, or curtain panels that can close. Are you trying to block an unsightly view? Café curtains may solve your woes. After you decide on a style, take accurate measurements. For outside-mount treatments, such as side panels and café curtains, measure from the outside of the window frame on one side to the outside of the frame on the other to determine width. To determine the length, measure from the top of the top trim to the bottom of the frame, under the apron. Some treatments, such as blinds and Roman shades, typically hang inside the window frame. To determine their width, measure inside the frame from one side to the other. For the length, measure from the top of the window, inside the frame, down the center of the window to the sill. For tab-top treatments, add 4–7 inches to the length to ensure that the treatment can be mounted high enough so only the wall, not the window frame, shows between the tabs or loops.

Add the trimmings.
Little details go a long way. Wood moldings from a home center can add architectural interest to a featureless room. A wallpaper border is architecture by the roll that's easy to install. After your backdrop is finished and the furnishings are in place, it's time to layer. Bring in pillows and throws for cozy comfort. A tassel hung on a doorknob and a pair of vintage reading glasses atop a stack of books are small details that can make a room complete.

Invest in advice.
The luxury of having an interior designer doesn't have to come with a big price tag. A one-hour consultation with a designer could help steer you away from costly mistakes. There are low-cost and no-cost options at your fingertips, too. Many stores have on-staff designers whose expertise you can tap while looking for furnishings and fabrics. Visit showhouses or model homes to see the latest in design. Even the displays at furniture stores can provide ideas, so take time to browse as you troll for inspiration.